This book is dedicated to "Miss Elise's Palestinian children who brought such love and life to this world and my life.

Elise Sjogren

I want to dedicate this to all the parents who want help in training their kids to live for the glory of God! May this make a big change in how your family lives life!

Bob Sjogren

Published by Mission Minded Publishers for UnveilinGLORY
© 2015 ❖ Sjogren and Sjogren
First Printing, 2015

No part of this book may be reproduced or transmitted in any form or by any means, electronic, or mechanical, including photocopying and recording, or by any information storage or retrieval system, except as may be expressly permitted in writing by the publisher. Requests for permission should be addressed in writing to:

    Mission Minded Publishers
    4663 Crown Hill Rd.
    Mechanicsville, VA 23111

ISBN: 978-0-9862066-3-4

To order additional copies, contact UnveilinGLORY at 804.781.0386

If you're new to *Cat and Dog Theology*, you're probably wondering, "What is this all about?" *Cat and Dog Theology* helps you see the differences between a God-centered and a people-centered Christianity. Both are found in the church. Its basis is found in a simple joke about the differences between a cat and a dog.

>A dog says, "You pet me, you feed me, you shelter me, you love me. **You** must be God."
>A cat says, "You pet me, you feed me, you shelter me, you love me, **I** must be God."

The joke asks a simple question. Do we live for God or does God live for us? Two different answers bring about two totally different Christian attitudes and lifestyles.

>Dogs pray to advance God's kingdom. Cats ask God to advance their kingdom.
>Dogs seek to make God famous. Cats ask God to make them famous.
>Dogs serve God. Cats expect God to serve them.
>Dogs ask, "What can I do for God?" Cats ask, "What can God do for me?"
>Dogs seek God's face. Cats seek His hand.
>Dogs primarily want God. Cats primarily want God's blessings.

These differences can change your entire Christianity. It can change the way you parent your child. It can change the way your child grows up. It can change everything! This book was specifically created to help you with the character development of the children in your life so that they might choose to live for the glory of God.

There are three ways you can use these cartoons:

1. Simply discuss the cartoon with your children and talk about the different attitudes.
2. Don't let them see the cartoon, but give them the scenario and tell them the "topic" at the top. Ask them how they think the Cat would respond and how they think the Dog would respond without letting them see the answer. Then discuss the differences between their answer and the answers given. (Who knows, their answer may be better than the cartoon book's answer itself!)
3. Before or after they read it, have them act out both the Dog's attitude and the Cat's attitude. In acting it out, they are much more likely to remember the differences between Cat attitudes and Dog attitudes. Feel free to ham it up with them!

Please note that we all wrestle with Cat attitudes (we call them "Cattitudes") in our lives. This is because we all have an old nature inside of us that has a natural tendency to rebel. Even the Apostle Paul wrestled with his old nature as an adult (see Romans 7:21-23.)

Though we seek perfection (Matthew 5:48), don't demand it from your children. Do expect to begin to see more Dog attitudes than Cat attitudes as they grow older. When the "Cattitudes" do reveal themselves, extend lots of grace to them (along with loving discipline if needed) knowing we all wrestle with Catness inside of us.

Always refer to Cartoon #1 repeatedly. Whether we are a Cat or a Dog, God loves us just the same. We can't earn God's love, this is why His love is unconditional. (We can earn rewards, but not love.) He loves us simply because He is love—and that's what love does!

We pray you'll have a fantastic time using this cartoon book to train your kids in Cat and Dog Theology! (Please note that *Cat and Dog Theology* is also in coloring book form, DVD form and other forms as well! See our website at: www.UnveilinGLORY.com/bookstore.)

When Cats and Dogs see someone being teased...

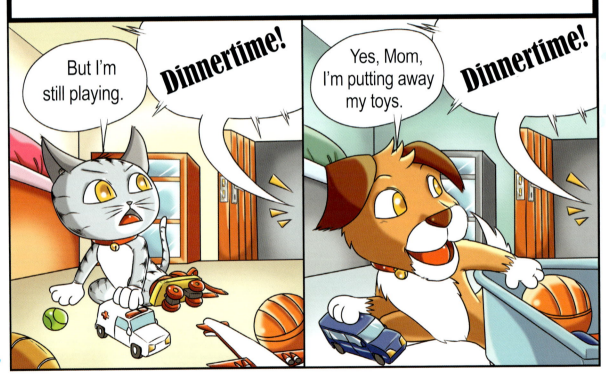

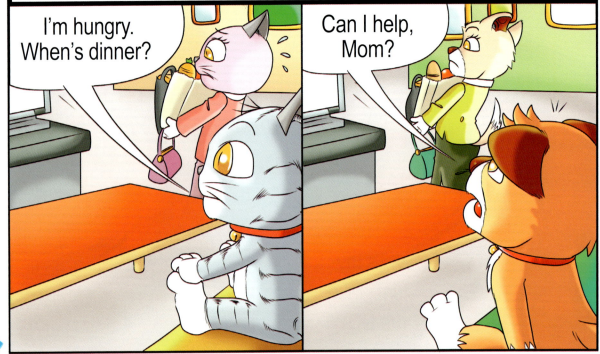

How Cats and Dogs make their bed...

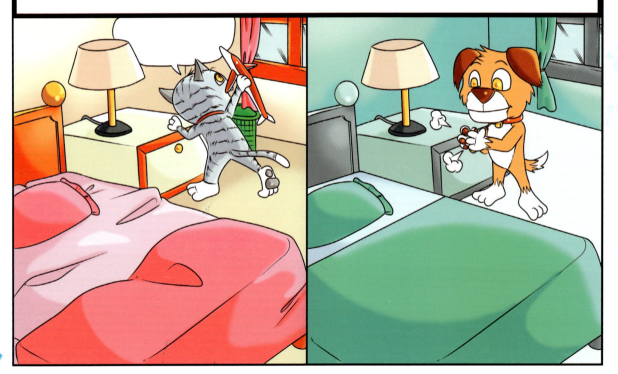

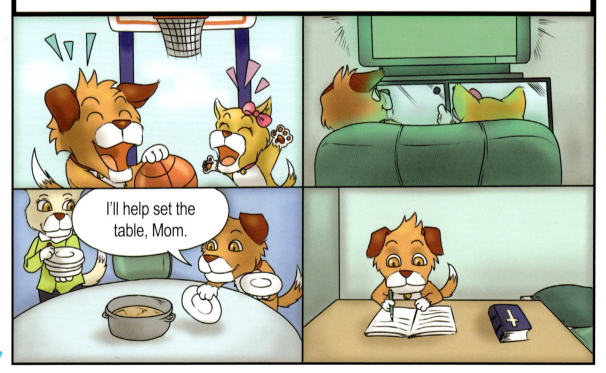

When Cats and Dogs are at a museum...

When Cats and Dogs get in line for a game...

When Cats and Dogs attend a group dinner...

When Mom isn't looking...

When their siblings drop a toy...

Where Cats and Dogs keep their dirty clothes...

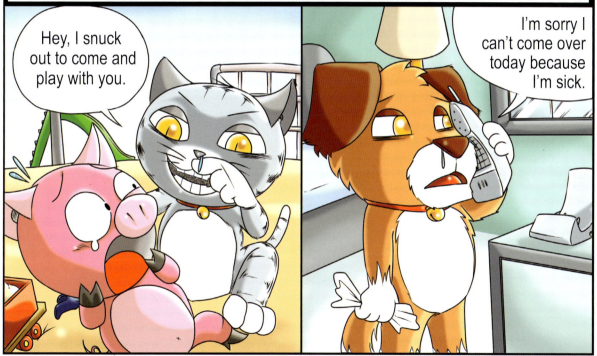

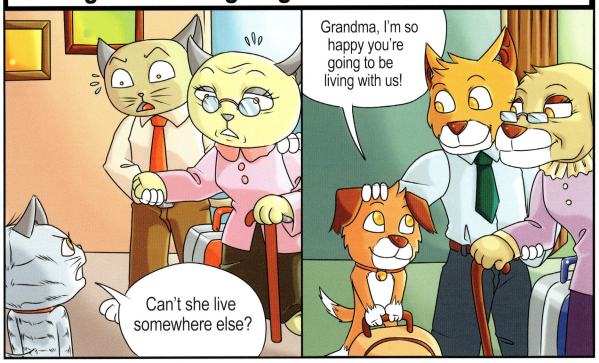

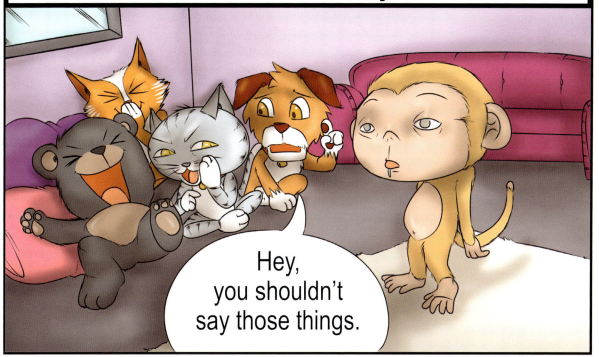

How Cats and Dogs Might Be Eternally Rewarded In Heaven

Thanks for reading
102 Differences Between Cats and Dogs for Kids!

Did you also know that UnveilinGLORY
has more materials for homeschoolers?
(They're also for Christians schools
and triple as great family devotions!)

Check out the latest at
www.CatandDogTheology.org—
or turn the page to find out more!

Written by a 14-year-old home schooled young lady, this brand new book takes you on a journey through 65 stories of how God has brought former Muslims, Hindus and Buddhists living in Asia to Himself.

Page after page will keep you on the edge of your seat as you read this book aloud to your children.

Each story is true and has happened since the year AD 2000. The people depicted in these stories are still alive today!

To order, go to:
   www.UnveilinGLORY.com/bookstore

For Grades 7-12

Year **1**

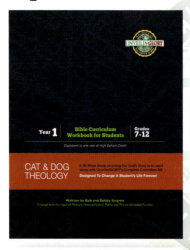

Life is not about us.
It is about living for
God's glory!

Year **2**

Once we know His glory,
we want to take it
to the nations!

For Grades 7-12

Year **3**

How we live our lives on earth prepares us for **eternal glory!**

Year **4**

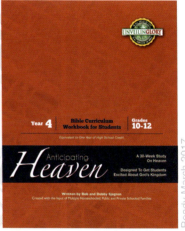

Understanding heaven gets us excited as God puts **His glory** on display—forever!

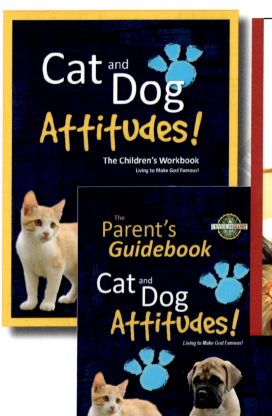

Our Elementary Kit!

For Kids Grades 1-5!